Alaska A-Z

By K.R. Nelson

Alaska A-Z, Standard edition

Copyright © 2021 all art and writing by K.R.Nelson. All rights reserved.
Except as permitted under the United States Copyright Act of 1976, no part
of this publication may be reproduced or distributed in any form or by any
means, or stored in a data base or retrieval system, without the prior written
permission of the author.

ISBN 978-1-716-20197-4
Imprint: Lulu.com

Alaska A-Z

This Book & Artwork is dedicated to my loving family, Ray Nelson, Jana Nelson, Nana, Papa and the awe inspiring place that has been my childhood home.
May these paintings serve to share just a little of Alaska's beauty and inspiration with your family, too.

-KRN

Is for **Arctic** Fox, playing in a thicket of **Alpine** Forget-Me-Nots.

Is for **Beluga** families, playing in our inlet waters.

Is for **Cranes** in the valley, large and poised with grace.

Is for **Dall** Sheep, found high along our mountain cliffs.

E Is for Bald **Eagle**s, sweeping up salmon in their mighty talons.

Is for **Fireweed**, growing tall and bright in the **fall**.

Is for this Kodiak **Grizzly** sow caring for her **growing** cub.

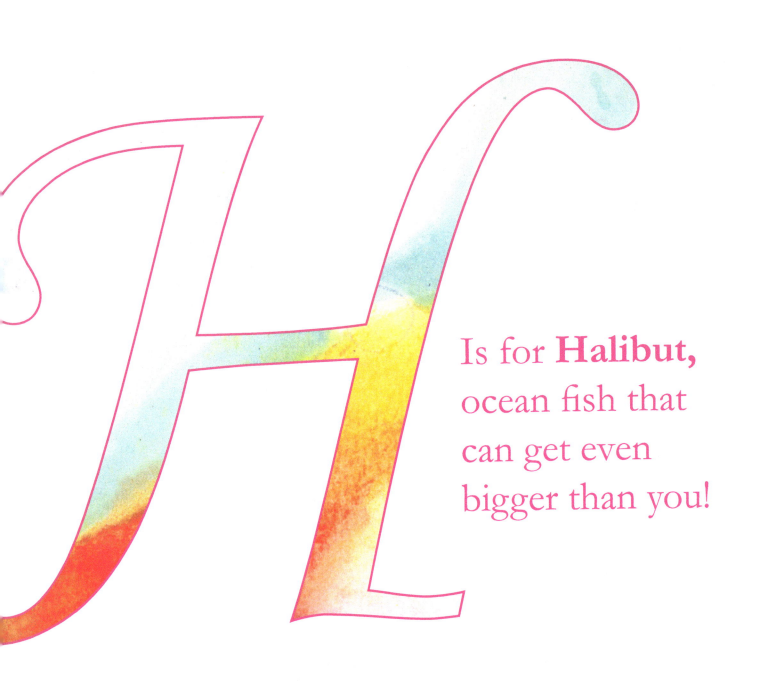

Is for **Halibut,** ocean fish that can get even bigger than you!

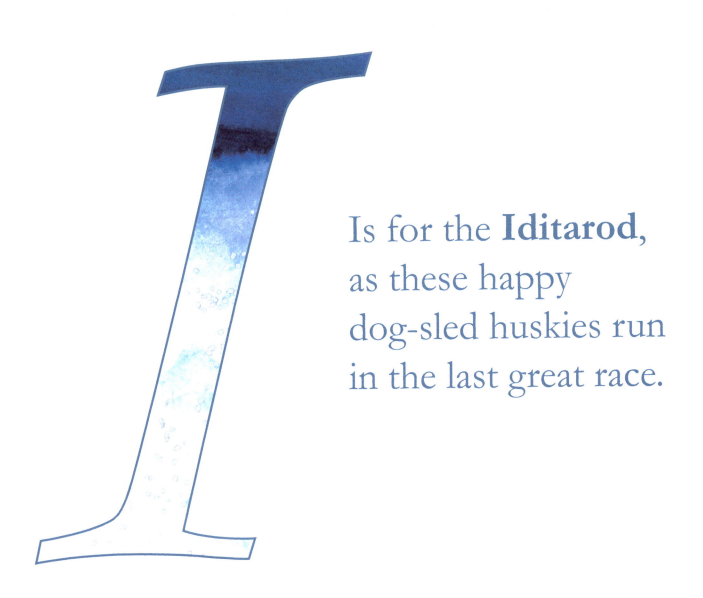

Is for the **Iditarod**, as these happy dog-sled huskies run in the last great race.

Is for the **Jellyfish** found in Whittier Harbor.

K

Is for the quiet **Kayak**, the best way to see our otter and ocean friends.

L Is for **Lynx**, agile and adapted to hunting in deep snow.

Is for **Momma Moose,** watching over her calves.

Is for the **Northern** Lights as they dance across our winter skies.

Is for **Orca**, our 'wolves' of the **open** seas.

Is for **Polar** Bear cubs, wrestling **playfully** with their mom.

Is for **Qiviut,** made from muskox wool, the warmest fiber on earth!

Is for **Raven**,
one of the cleverest and curious corvids.

Is for **Snowshoe** Hare, huddled in the winter tundra **snow**.

Is for **Tongass** National Forest, a northern temperate rain forest that is home to many endangered and rare species.

Is for the **Ursa** constellations.

The Big Dipper points to the North Star (Polaris) in the Little Dipper's handle.

Is for the Alaska **Violet,** found along the Aleutian chain.

W Is for our Gray **Wolf** packs, howling their songs to one another.

Is for **eXtra** large, because everything in Alaska is huge!

Is for the **Yukon** River, with bears fishing for Salmon as they **run** up its **rapids**.

Is for this **Zodiak**™ boat, used to get a closer look at our glaciers and harbor creatures.